ONE RED EYE

Poems by Kirsten Dierking

Excerpt from "Ars Poetica?" by Czeslaw Milosz from
Bells in Winter, 1978 (The Ecco Press). Reprinted by
permission of HarperCollins Publishers, Inc.

Library of Congress Cataloging-in-Publication Data

Dierking, Kirsten, 1962-
One red eye: poems / Kirsten Dierking.
p. cm.
ISBN 0-930100-59-X
1. Rape victims—Poetry. I. Title.

PS3604.154 054 2001
811'.6—dc21   2001016833

Holy Cow! Press titles are distributed to the trade by
Consortium Book Sales & Distribution, 1045 Westgate Drive,
Saint Paul, Minnesota 55114. Our books are available
through all major library distributors, including
Bookpeople and Small Press Distribution.
For inquiries, please write to:

Holy Cow! Press
Post Office Box 3170
Mount Royal Station
Duluth, MN 55803

ONE RED EYE

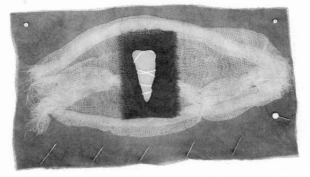

Poems by Kirsten Dierking

HOLY COW! PRESS · DULUTH MINNESOTA · 2001

ACKNOWLEDGEMENTS

GRATEFUL ACKNOWLEDGEMENT is made to the editors and publishers of the following journals and anthologies in which some of these poems first appeared: *ArtWord Quarterly, The Aurora, The Fargo ArtForum, The Lake Region Review, The Mankato Poetry Review, The Minnesota Poetry Calendar (1997, 1998, 2000), Mother Superior, O Finland, Poetry Motel, Rag Mag, Shout, Sidewalks, Sing Heavenly Muse!, Spout, Water-Stone, and Xanadu.*

I wish to express profound gratitude for the love, wisdom, support, and good humor of my friends and family. Special thanks to Floyd and Nancy Paurus, Robin Paurus, Leslie Rentmeester, Dianne Gray, and Kay Korsgaard. Thanks to the students, staff and instructors who make the M.A.L.S. program at Hamline University so extraordinary. I am grateful to writers/teachers Deborah Keenan, Mary Rockcastle, and Roseann Lloyd for inspiration and encouragement. Thanks also to Jim Perlman, publisher, Lisa McKhann, artist, and the staff and student workers in the University of St. Thomas libraries. For my husband, Patrick Dierking, all my love, your generous spirit made the writing of this book possible.

For more information on *One Red Eye:* www.dierking.net

For Patrick

CONTENTS

FORFEIT SIGNS

IN PACE WITH THE PAST

FOREWORD

IT WAS THE SUMMER OF 1983 and I had just turned twenty-one. Less than enthusiastic about the large, impersonal university I'd been attending for the past three years, I decided to look around for a smaller school, finally settling on a college in northern Arizona. I based my decision on two things: the promise of a shorter winter, and the fact that the school hosted a branch of my sorority, allowing me to live in a sorority apartment rather than a dormitory.

In August I packed up my car and followed the highway into the desert. Everything was strange, the landscape, the distance I was traveling from home. My apprehensions over making new friends and finding my way around a new city were outweighed, however, by the prospect of making my first real foray into an independent life. Just before I left, my parents gave me the gift of a gray wool suit, a chic, business-like outfit, and I pictured myself wearing it as I returned on the airplane at Christmas, clearly a sophisticated woman of the world.

Instead, I found myself returning home less than a week later, physically battered, perpetually terrified, one of my eyes a bright scarlet, the whites filled with blood. A transformation had occurred, and the student who left for Arizona, the one who thought she was strong, believed she was lucky, the girl who walked alone after dark, had vanished forever. In her place was a broken creature who trembled constantly, screamed in her sleep, flinched when she was touched. A victim of rape and attempted murder.

With these poems, I have done my best to share, both literally and emotionally, the truth of this experience. The first part of the book tells specifically of the crime, the second part of the years spent drifting, and almost drowning, in the aftermath. The third section reflects, I hope, the emergence of a new woman—altered, yet resilient, someone who finds enough strength in family roots to accept the past and walk into a happier future.

When I first started writing, I had no intention of using my own experience with sexual assault as material. But the more I wrote, the more I realized that silence on the topic was impossible. I simply couldn't speak candidly about my perceptions of the world without including this experience. It changed the way I think, walk, talk, see, feel; it affected every aspect of my life. Trying to write without acknowledging the taint of violence would have taken constant vigilance and continual camouflage, and allowed only a partial voice. As a poet, I wanted a whole voice. As a crime victim, I wanted a true accounting; this book is the only testimony I am ever likely to give in this case.

There are other, less personal reasons why silence on the subject of rape is an unacceptable alternative. A few weeks after I returned home from Arizona, an acquaintance there wrote to me that nothing about the assault was ever mentioned in the school newspaper, and that she found this appalling. I was living in such a dull emotional fog at the time, I found it hard to summon up either anger or concern over the issue, and never replied to her letter. I didn't really think of it again until about a year ago, when I was playing around with a library database that stores old newspaper articles. On impulse, I decided to look for my story. I typed in the college name, the keyword rape, and entered the year 1983. What showed up on the screen wasn't my story, but a UPI column dated October, 1983, approximately six weeks after I had been assaulted. It told of a female student who was attacked and raped on the same campus, by a man who subdued her by "putting her in a choke hold." As you will see from reading this book, it seems quite possible this woman and I share the same rapist.

I wonder about her, what she has suffered over the years. I wonder if her suffering could have been prevented. Would she have been walking alone late at night if she'd known about me? In this case, silence seems to have largely benefited one person, and that person was a criminal, intent on hunting women.

Today, I am stronger, lucky enough to have overcome much of the terrible distress that kept me quiet for so many years after the crime. Now that I am capable of speaking, I think I must. Maybe if I can share this story, it will help people better understand the true ferocity and disastrous repercussions of sexual assault. Maybe it will help a victim of violence feel less alone. Maybe it will help dissipate the cloud of unwarranted shame that is the burden of so many rape victims. If this book can do something, anything positive, it might imbue the whole tragic experience with meaning.

I am always looking for meaning in the wake of a senseless crime.

—*Kirsten Dierking*

ONE RED EYE

*"The purpose of poetry is to remind us
how difficult it is to remain just one person,
for our house is open, there are no keys in the doors,
and invisible guests come in and out at will."*

Ars Poetica?, Czeslaw Milosz

ARIZONA DESERT

The Buick cruises through bands
of color, blue-bright crayon

streaked at top, orange crags
like candy-corn on a cloudless sky.

Impersonal light, blastingly white,
shimmers the gravel. No trees,

no shelter. No signs or portents,
except for maybe the desert itself,

the weather prediction for thunder
and heat, the tarmac lying ahead,

submissive. A cross of roads
offers up the illusion of choice,

but you've made your decision.
If momentum was ever reversible,

you've passed that point.

GETTING READY TO MEET THE SISTERS

The oxford shirt is supposed to say
instinctive taste. The brand but

not designer jeans, faded to look
like unplanned ease. Earrings,

watchband, make-up, belt, all medium
length and width and thickness, aimed

at pleasing whatever they think.
I practice my smile again in the mirror.

Hair's not bad, but the grin is slipping
toward supplication, like Raggedy Ann's,

when I'd pull up her dress
and expose the secret heart on her chest.

THE ALLOTTED ROOMMATE

Sunny revs hard, a racing Ferrari,
her tongue burning rubber, her lips

peeling squeals from visible gums.
She says we're together because we're

left-over. She says her boyfriend's
a Pike, that's a frat. She says

the Pikes have RADICAL parties.
They're, like, FOR SURE, the most

popular frat. Is the Flashdance
soundtrack to DIE FOR or WHAT?

Disco blares from the biggest
boombox I've ever seen, and

Sunny swivels her motorized hips.
I realize there is no finishing flag.

Her tires are light with internal air,
her supply of gas, inexhaustible.

INITIATION

The thing I keep
is the chapter's motto;
Grace and Strength.

I am twenty-one
and wearing white.
Right to the ends

of my bones, my fists,
I am reckless with hope,
thoughtless with power.

Smug with strength
and lazy with grace
in my white linen dress.

But luck is like
the rose I'm holding,
transient. Luck is like

the candle I light,
flickering. My future
is like the ruby badge

a sister pins over my
heart. Red as blood
and as close as tomorrow.

SUNNY SAYS PLEASE

A knock on the door.
It's Sunny and GOD!

She's GOT to get ready,
the Pikes are having

a party, a BIG one.
Nibbles a nail so

nonchalant, I know
something's up.

She guesses she'll
probably stay there

tonight. Of course,
they're in love, if

THAT makes a difference.
I say I don't care.

Stay a long time.
Really. Feel free.

Sunny shrieks YES!
She KNEW I'd be cool!

Says will I leave
the door unlocked.

'Cause they might
have a fight. 'Cause

she lost her key.
'Cause it costs

twenty bucks to get
a new key, like she

HAS twenty bucks,
like she'd spend it

on a key if she had it,
so will I, please?

Be nice and leave
the door unlocked?

Sure, I can do that.
I think about the

missing keys, open
doors of my freshman

dorm. Everything
always turned out

fine. I want to be
nice. Sunny says

AWESOME! THANKS,
like a MILLION!

And I go back to
reading my book.

Untroubled. Mostly.
I leave it unlocked.

DYING

There's a hand on my mouth,
so I'm dreaming, right,
the pillow, the sheet,
the dark, night...

An arm at my throat.
Something... God,
has got me, grabbing,
dragging, hold on,
I crash to the floor,
there is *somebody here*,
is it me screaming?

SHUT UP OR I'LL KILL YOU
the arms lock tight,
screaming, screaming,
SHUT UP OR I'LL KILL YOU
screaming, clawing,
kicking, ripping,
dizzy as I hit the wall.

Cloth on my face,
a glove finds my mouth,
seals too tight and I
can't breathe.

Someone, Sunny? Please,
Sunny, stands at the door,
fades away in a brutal
trick, no one to help.

Strike with my leg,
and the bed screeches
across the floor,
the canvas hand
covers my mouth and I
can't breathe. I can
bite. I sink my teeth,
for a second it moves,
then back again, skin now,
crushing my jaw,
withholding my air.

I CAN'T BREATHE!
I raise my arms
for a final claw.
Human hair?
The weight of a body
slides on top and
I can't breathe.

I have nothing left.
I can't breathe.

Just one more breath.
The world has stopped
for one more breath,

all I want,
I'm watching
the drawer of my
wooden dresser,
the common, vivid,
grain of the wood,

and the world moves on
without that breath.

I am going
to die.

I am so
calm.

Funny, really,
without any air.
A dresser, curious,
not so painful,

surprising, yes,
I would have thought,

last sight,

not a dresser.

Not this room.

Not yet.

NEW WORLD

There has never been a better moment.
My mind opens and I can breathe.

Look at my face and I'll kill you.
Fine. Just let me breathe.

Flesh on flesh, in and out, I start
to hope, in and out, but I can breathe.

He's fucking me now. Most rape victims live.
Look at my face and I'll kill you, bitch.

Breathing raspy, rashly speaking,
swear to God when you're done you'll leave.

I swear to God. Pumping away.
I press my cheek to the floor and breathe.

Believe in God? *No.* He laughs.
But his dick goes soft, he says he's sorry

Sorry I couldn't keep it up longer.
Courteous lover, sincerely abashed,

I just keep breathing.

FINISHED

Zip, the teeth of his fly bite shut.
Look and I'll kill you.

Okay, I don't look.
Get up or I'll kill you.

Okay, I try. Legs are shaky, but a
prod from his foot and I make it up.

Go stand by the window.
Okay. Six steps. I make it. Stop.

Turn and I'll kill you.
I stare at the curtains, my back so naked

I wonder if maybe he'll shoot me now,
though that seems unfair.

I wait at the curtains, and wait.
Nothing. I turn. Nothing. I'm all

alone. I believe I'm alive.

FOUR-SEVENTEEN A.M.

Now what? Lights first.
A voice from the bathroom,
vaguely familiar,
"Why don't you clean up?"

It sounds like she wants
to take care of this person,
whoever it is, in the mirror,
bleeding.

She (it's a woman)
scrubs at the scratches,
the mottled necklace
of darkening bruises,
and now she's looking
through one red eye,
the pupil rolling
in clouds of blood.

She's pissed herself.
But the well-trained
voice says not to shower,
so the wet with urine
pajama top gets tossed
on the floor,
"Now find yourself
some decent clothes."

"Straighten this room."
But the wounded woman,
feeble and weak, can't
budge the bed, she
leaves it askew, piles
the quilt somebody's mother
gave her for Christmas
onto the bed.

Now what?
"Now go to the phone
and call for help."
But she can't think how
the telephone works.
Just punches at numbers,
nobody home.

"I'll handle this."
The voice obligingly
pushes the fingers,
the voice says something
that sounds like help,
help for the eye
staring back bleeding,
the damaged ghost
in the bathroom mirror.

BACKWARD IN RED

In the waiting room a green sun
settles cold light on cracked
orange chairs. My one good eye

is matching faces to thoughtless
words. A "sister" says, could we
play down the sorority thing?

A few squeeze my hand as they
run unbroken, gallop for home,
through double glass doors that

spell emergency backward in red.
I stay, defective, with new
instructors; the Victim's Aid,

the nurse who tells me it's
time to go in and stick my
cold feet up in the stirrups.

RIDE TO THE BATTERED WOMEN'S SHELTER

The sun shines in Flagstaff
all of the time, but the people
aren't warm, cardboard dolls,

I watch them walking an alien
street, they don't know I'm
living an eight day week.

They don't know I'm watching
through splintered eyes.
They don't know how the sun,

slanting in rivers of cold-
hearted light, hurts the heart
of the eighth day crowd.

A pedestrian crosses the
listing road. My nails
slide down the distorted day.

How hard to say I will not
go crazy when the sun keeps
jagging down like a joke.

A DAY IN SHELTER

She's sharing her smokes and we have to smile
when both our hands shake so bad,
it takes two minutes to get one lit.

She's just nineteen. Her father said,
she's her husband's problem. Problem is,
for the past two years, her husband's

been bringing the guys around, for a group
bang on Saturday nights. "When they're drunk,"
she explains. "Tell and I'll kill you,

he always said." I nod because I believe
in these words. It's the reason I'm here.
I tell her keep talking, anything so

I don't have to think. The shelter worker,
our Victim's Aid, brings herbal tea,
the normal world in a cracked yellow cup.

I say to Janice, "You left?" "I left.
Just one morning. Just like that. I left
everything. Photo album, Grandma's quilt,

my boots, my toothbrush, my silver earrings."
What I like about Janice is how she reads minds.
She knows my destruction is still too fresh

to piece together. She knows I'm in danger
of disbelieving, or somehow thinking
I am alone. She's giving me context.

Janice says, "One morning I just walked out
the door. I was sore, you know, moving
slow, I was too tired to brush my hair,

jeans and a shirt, I forgot about shoes,
I'm praying so hard he won't wake up,
but a door slams and out he comes.

Rubbing his eyes, bitch, I'll kill you,
then he says, bitch, I'll shoot you."
My bloody eye and my bruised lips

are good enough signs of my sympathy.
Janice says, "I couldn't run. It felt like fate,
or a movie scene. Is she going to escape,

is she going to die, yes, no, a flip
of the coin." She takes a drag on her
cigarette. Her next words enter the room

in a sigh of smoke. "He shot at my back
as I walked down the drive. He was either
still drunk, or just being nice, he missed

by a mile. Still, it seemed like a very
long walk. When I got to the road, I

stuck out my thumb. I've been here now

for the past three months." She reaches
again for a cigarette and her hands shake.
It takes two minutes to get one lit.

...

Janice offers to lend me her comb and I wonder
where she learned to be kind. Asks me if
she's sitting too close. "We're careful about

the touching here, we know what it's like, a brush
of the hand." Yes, I nod, now part of a group
where a touch can feel like a gunshot sounds.

...

This keeps getting harder. The shelter worker
says I should call my parents now. I resist
for an hour. I know when I call, things will

change. I want to stay with that cracked
yellow cup, and daylight forever, and Janice
who doesn't sit too close. But finally I call.

I think I begin with, "I'm in trouble."
Even now I can't say what words I used.
I remember everything else, but this.

•••

The police come, the only men allowed
in the house, familiar with this room,
these stories, they settle into their favorite chairs.

I tell them how I ended up here, needing
shelter. Describe to two strangers rape,
erection, specific positions. Suffocation.

I get through my story, I do because Janice
gets through hers. Later, I say my Dad
will be taking me home, Janice stares

at how simple this miracle sounds.
She lets me give him our secret address,
but balks at letting him into the house.

•••

I watch my father, confused on the street,
the shelter worker trying to explain
why men aren't allowed, the glut of fear.

My dad pleading, "But I'm her *father.*"
There is no explaining two worlds to my dad.
There is no explaining Janice's father to my father.

Janice decides she wants to meet him.
We go out on the walk, Janice says hi,
my dad says hello, gives her his most

distracted smile. She whispers to me,
"My God, you're lucky," and suddenly
I find my new context. My throat bruised,

but still breathing. My dad waiting,
wanting to help. Janice, homeless, but
warm enough in the women's shelter.

Luck is a charm you ward against things
that could have been worse. When Janice
and I say good-bye, we don't touch.

We say, "Good luck."

PRIVATE CRIME

Fingerprint dust is metallic gray
like soot rolling out from a cunning
chimney. Sticking to doorjambs,
searching for alien, feral grooves.

I'm sitting inside a ring of police
who work inside the daffodil yellow
crime scene tape. First we have
a broken chain. A tiny diamond.

"Yours?" "Mine." Dropped and labeled
in plastic bags. The quilt my mother
gave me for Christmas gets bagged and
tagged and shipped off for testing.

"His?" they're asking. So I edge
over, it's there on the floor, right
where I tore it off with my teeth.
Dirty glove, fingers curled in a

filthy claw, something inside once,
prowling, flexing. It plays dead now
and I say, "His." Grace and Strength.
(But somehow that glove

crawls from the bag, I find it later
all over the country, lying in gutters,
sly on a sidewalk, storing the past
in hundreds of angry, abandoned fists.)

THE D.A. HAS POLISHED NAILS

I.

Tap, tap, tap,
her fingers on

that handsome desk,
diplomas dusted,

Too bad, she says,
you didn't manage

a look at his face.
You're not giving me

much to work with
you know.

II.

Fingers tapping.
What color was he?

The crackling orange
of fire licking the edge

of the bedclothes.
The scarlet of rages,

fevers and scratches.
The silver of knives.

The brassy bad luck
of lightning strikes,

the grizzled rumble
of lingering thunder

long after it's over.
The color of bruises

or cross-stitched scars
or a hemorrhaged eye.

III.

Tap. Tap. Tap.
You're not giving me

much to work with
you know.

IV.

No one's been scraping
under her nails

for a skin sample.

MIDNIGHT, ROOM 26

At the Holiday Inn the lights are on,
the TV blasting, I won't have silence,

or darkness, breeding. I shut my eyes.
Someone steps too close to the bed.

My scream an indiscriminate bite, my
scramble frantic to reach a safe corner.

Dad backs off. I'm sorry for making him
watch me hurt, but I can't sleep, this

first of a thousand vigilant nights
in harshly lit rooms, years of guilt,

apologies no one says they expect,
but I feel I should make. For exposing

their soft-focus dreams to the light.

DIFFERENT ROAD HOME

Sunshine finally feels right today.
Tires humming, road signs marking

the miles required for safer breathing.
The car feels clean, the roof is empty,

nothing clings to the wheels, the hood,
the trunk stays clear of all dark objects.

The back seat's filled with mascot bears
and good-luck gifts, but I check it again

in the rearview mirror. Attentive to
shadows. And man, I can drive, thinking

the harm isn't hidden in me. But that,
of course, is just the morning. The sun

shining falsely. The driving away.

RECURRING THEMES

Three weeks later.
Three states away.

Inside my parked car
when the news comes on,

"Sorority girl found
strangled to death."

I lock the doors.
Tell and I'll kill you.

I shouldn't have told.
Now he's out there,

waiting. He's killed
the wrong girl.

Adrenaline cracks my
heart on my ribs.

Can't move my legs.
Can't catch my breath.

I stay locked up
the windows shut

the sun beating in
for over two hours.

People walk by
like normal life.

And the late night news
told how she strangled,

his hands a nightmare
uniquely her own.

I MIGHT HAVE DREAMED THIS

For a short time after
the rape, I found I could

move things. Energy birds
swarmed from my brain.

With a witch's sense
of abandoned physics,

I set dolls rolling.
Back and forth. Like a

breathing sound.

Using only my night-powered
eyes, I pushed the lamp

to the dresser's edge.
I buried the mirrors

in avalanches of freshly
laundered underpants.

I never slept.

I did all these things
lying down.

THE PLEASURE OF SAFETY

That, in the course of justice, none of us
Should see salvation: we do pray for mercy;
*   Portia, Merchant of Venice,*
*   William Shakespeare*

I imagine it down to the shoes
I'm wearing on the witness stand.

A faceless defendant. A quick
conviction. Bars and chains.

How this didn't happen. He was
never caught. So I also imagine

an eye for an eye. He breaks in
my house and this time I'm ready.

I've got a gun. I'm going to kill
him. First, I give my testimony:

For all the days I've been too
afraid to leave the house. For

nights I can never spend alone.
For the time I woke up kicking

and clawing the man I love,
hearing your voice call me bitch.

For sheets soaked in adrenaline
sweat. For walks I can't take.

For thinking I must have deserved
your touch. For crippling years

of heart-sick fear that made me unsure
which way I should point the gun.

Now that he's here, I know
who's to blame. I aim for the skull.

Pull the trigger. Watch his head
blown the fuck apart, his blood on

the walls like a proffered flower
of red appeasement. It makes me

smile. You know this is not
who I wanted to be. But late at night,

startled by every noise in the house,
this is the ending that guarantees

sleep. I *crave* good sleep. Don't
count on mercy from women forever.

FORFEIT SIGNS

AMERICAN GIRLS

We were sitting beside each other with a metal wall
between us, in the bathroom of some latest club,
and we went in looking real good: American girls
from double garages and tennis courts.

But once we got hiding behind those doors, we wouldn't
shut up. She said: I never thought life would be so hard.
She meant we got our college degrees and trendy skirts
and a past with a man who grooved little girls. We got
new cars and import beer, and we still got rape and a
bleeding eye.

When we unlocked those toilet doors, we were scared
too soft, so we sprayed our hair in savage designs
and then we looked sharp as a close survival.

I HURT

The windowshade spins
relentlessly down.

In one gritting day,
hot tar encircles

your vital organs.
You can't wake up.

You lay very still.
You hurt very quiet.

Ashes grow rank
in the roots of your hair.

Your body succumbs
to the drag of your eyes.

You try to vent
your pressurized heart;

a drink, or a drug.
The next day you can

wash out your hair.
The next day you can

enter the store.
The next day you can

feel it seep.
You draw the tar

scalding through
the wick of your hands

and just when you think
about reaching for help,

your hands finish softly
burning away.

BROKEN

Yesterday, I would have been brought down
by something sharp and opportunistic.

Predators smelling the sweat I woke up in
as lethargy. Scavengers reading my dirty

hair, the low swing of my head and shoulders
as forfeit signs. Tainted, I would have

trailed the herd, my unfit prints like an
aromatic dinner-bell, the degenerate spiral

path of my thoughts a clear concession to
carnivores. Yesterday, I was too sick

to do anything else but accept the wolves.
I might even have kissed their fur.

TRANSMUTATION

In the morning,
in the mirror,

white strands of hair
drifted in and out

the teeth of my comb.
Filaments of snow

framed my face
with alienness.

Unsettling how
I had suddenly started

to look so much
like somebody else.

First, I cut
a tendril of color,

to not forget.
The lock inert

in a fetal curl
on the countertop,

the subtle trace
of soil inherent

in body fragments.
I threw it away.

Next, I bought
a solution for dyeing,

stained my head
with the caustic scent

of laboratories,
replicating

the only reflection
I'd ever known.

That night,
I woke up startled,

to a room I had painted,
a quilt I had chosen,

a picture I framed
with my own hands,

and I was a stranger,
owner of nothing,

not even my dark hair.

DELACROIX'S VERSION

Ophelia hangs still tangible
in a pool so green it drifts

between a languid peace and a
dead calm. She is holding onto

a branch, her mouth passive,
but well above her liquid line

of obligation. Maybe she'll
float for one afternoon, drag

herself out, but this is only
a dream, unframed. The branch

she is holding is not even
as thick as her arm. Her hair

is already weaving in weeds,
her dress is draped serenely

with sleep. Even the tree's
critical limbs are cracking now,

urging her to accept her immersion,
while she is still lovely,

surrendering.

HOLBEIN'S FAVOUR FOR ANNE OF CLEVES

Famous for his brutal portraits, he painted her pleasant.
Maybe they talked as he painted, maybe she smiled, whatever
the slip, this view of Anne reached

Henry the Eighth, and he held the portrait first up close, fingered
the frame, shut one eye, squinted and giggled and said
she'll do, and ordered her up

so they loaded her up and shipped her over and holy mary
mother of god she looked like a horse and Henry gagged
at her sturdy flanks, but maybe Henry was fond of horses

he let her live and called her his sister and set her up
in the countryside, and forgot all about the Flanders mare
he had almost mounted. Apparently Anne

was happy enough and talked to herself with her foreign tongue,
walked in the garden, patted her mismatched party of dogs,
and generally acted as she had been painted.

MERCY BY DEFAULT

Revenge these days sounds mildly
sweet, nostalgic like a Christmas

carol, a homecoming game. Used
to picture myself a blasting horror

of retribution. I had a gun.
Marksmanship was never the problem.

But unbelievably, years go by.
Nights, increasingly, nightmare free.

I'd like to say some holy bolt of
divine forgiveness took the itch

from my trigger finger, but really,
it's only hate fatigued by the

aging process. A creeping wrinkle
of acquiescence. A latent taste

for resignation, and soothing,
bland, unsalted soup.

AUBADE FOR A LONG HATRED

I am awake
like stepping

out of a bath,
and coating myself

in the lightest drops
of scent of calm

the lake makes
with mist rising

just after dawn.
I am like a drink

from the mist,
cooling all night

against the lake,
and now the haze

goes up slow,
like rising bread,

like a weather balloon.
I am weaving my hands

through mist,
like dressing myself

in a humid robe,
and damp and fresh

and warm and sleepy
I rock my mind

like a wave holding
a white feather.

I am starting
to think

at the speed
of forgiveness.

HOW TO FISH HAPPY

The noise of halcyon blue rises sharp from
the lake when Robin turns the motor off.

We slept late, so we're dropping our lines
at high noon, when no one has ever caught

a fish. We cast silver lures with red ruby
eyes that refract July, the loons are diving

like black feather jets, I keep forgetting
how to be nervous and how to hurt.

Happiness licks the fiberglass boat with
wave after wave of fresh-water lake.

Gulls doze. Nothing is biting.

IN PACE WITH THE PAST

FLOATING

I slip into the July arms of Long Lake,
my chin pressed to the red vinyl pillow,

my hands weaving like ghosts underwater.
Tiny pan fish trail along, in love with

the pearls of my water-soaked nails. A
fish jumps, splashing rings that smooth

themselves in absorbent blue, spread
toward stilling, and never happened.

Time dissolves in water-color. I flash
like the shine of silver fins against

the clock of the counting world, I am
always floating, tactile and warm, and

never happened.

MAIN STREET

Like a silver lighthouse,
the grain elevator draws

your car from the lapping
prairie. A buffalo faded

high on the side says
Welcome Back to Buffalo Lake.

Where the lake was drained
so long ago, soil was money.

Where the park was built
so long ago, they put up

swings for new generations.
You drive by vacant,

startled storefronts,
decades late for closing time.

Roll through irrelevant
four-way stops. Turn beyond

the catatonic wooden arms
of the railroad crossing,

into a new construction
zone at the nursing home.

Here you find them. Reeling
with stories so crisp and vibrant,

you almost forget
they are all past tense.

Walk your grandfather down
the linoleum tiled

new main street. Wave
to the neighbors waiting inside

their numbered doors.
Look out the window.

Watch as all the buffalo ghosts
stampede out of town.

BLACK SUIT

Too hot to be standing exposed
on the prairie, in a black suit,
the sun flashing mica from every

headstone. When a single ribbon
of humid wind catches my hair;
pungent with distance, scented

with age. Carries the relic
of grass-fire smoke, a dust cloud
churned by buffalo hooves. A balmy

aroma of sweet corn silk. A tang
of berries in strawberry leaves.
The heavy honey of lily bouquets.

The breeze moves on, slippery as
minutes, careless as time. Leaves
vacant, dull, unbreathable air.

The wind has stolen the tinge
of garden that always flavored
my grandfather's skin.

WHAT IS REQUIRED

Easy to do what is required
of the moment. Today I'll be
a pallbearer.

My mother says not to worry,
he was so frail, he can
only be light.

No one says the weight of a
casket, or just how far
we have to walk.

I wear sensible shoes.
The rain holds off. Still,
I find myself needing

both my hands, and then,
at the grave, no one says
how to let go.

MIDDLE-AGED JANUS

At the service I thought of my grandfather young.
Twenty. Sturdy. His capable hands on the reins
of the horses, the same way I felt when I drove
in my Mustang, sure of the value in acceleration.

I felt it then; age occurring. Clinical, dry.
Not too scary. Like the sound of snipping
when you close your eyes and the barber moves
the silver scissors against your skin. A self-image,
light as hair, falling away. After the funeral,

I tried to detect the exact effect of the cut
in a mirror. It looked like me, only tired and wearing
appropriate dress. But I had a new angle, like my eyes
had twisted a bit in the skull, and now they could see
over my shoulder. The view looking back
stretched as long as the future.

SNOW WALKER

Snow walker under
a featherbed sky

unstuffing itself
with goose's down.

Legs swing at a
reindeer gait,

reindeer mitts
direct the flakes.

Hoof-print boots
stamp transient signs

on a shifting surface,
drifting with rifts.

No people. No voices.
Only the houses,

watching unsleeping,
their eyes like

windows, attune
to the spell

of a Sami painting
silence with snow.

JOIK
(Sami Song)

Today I found my roots in Lapland.
Reason for the intrinsic scent

of snow in my blood. Reason why
my heart beats too soft and slow

for business or traffic. Why I
breathe better with deer and dogs,

feel electric spirits in animal eyes,
see at night with my dreaming mind.

My hair is dark to make me known
in a blanched land. My sturdy bones

are white to remember arctic frost.
Sami. Reindeer. Midnight sun.

Watch me walk in pace with the past,
perfectly dressed in my own skin.

KIRSTEN DIERKING was born in Minneapolis, and grew up in Minnesota, Toronto, and Colorado. She received a bachelor's degree in International Affairs and History from the University of Colorado, and a master's degree in creative writing from Hamline University in St. Paul, Minnesota. She lives with her husband in Arden Hills, Minnesota.